W9-BWS-779

Ocean Sunfish

A Buddy Book by
Deborah Coldiron

ABDO
Publishing Company

UNDERWATER WORLD

VISIT US AT
www.abdopublishing.com

Published by ABDO Publishing Company, 8000 West 78th Street, Edina, Minnesota 55439.

Copyright © 2009 by Abdo Consulting Group, Inc. International copyrights reserved in all countries. No part of this book may be reproduced in any form without written permission from the publisher. Buddy Books™ is a trademark and logo of ABDO Publishing Company.

Printed in the United States.

Coordinating Series Editor: Sarah Tieck
Contributing Editor: Michael P. Goecke
Graphic Design: Deborah Coldiron
Cover Photograph: Mike Johnson Marine Natural History Photography:
Mike Johnson/earthwindow.com
Interior Photographs/Illustrations: AP Images (page 28); Mike Johnson Marine Natural History Photography: Mike Johnson/earthwindow.com (page 7, 9, 11, 23, 24, 25, 30); Minden Pictures: Norbert Wu (page 17); PeterArnold.com: Aldo Brando/Peter Arnold Inc. (page 19); Photos.com (page 5, 18, 19, 21, 26, 27)

Library of Congress Cataloging-in-Publication Data

Coldiron, Deborah.
    Ocean sunfish / Deborah Coldiron.
      p. cm.-- (Underwater world)
    Includes index.
    ISBN 978-1-60453-135-0
    1. Mola (Genus)--Juvenile literature. I. Title.

    QL638.M64C65 2009
    597'.64 -- dc22

                                    2008005049

Table Of Contents

The World Of Ocean Sunfish . . . 4

A Closer Look 10

Three Species 14

A Growing Ocean Sunfish 16

Family Connections 18

Dinnertime 20

A World Of Danger 24

Fascinating Facts 28

Learn And Explore 30

Important Words 31

Web Sites 31

Index 32

The World Of Ocean Sunfish

Every living creature needs water. Some animals not only need water, they live in it, too.

Scientists have found more than 250,000 kinds of plants and animals living underwater. And, they believe there could be one million more! The ocean sunfish is one animal that makes its home in this underwater world.

Water covers 70 percent of Earth's surface.

Ocean sunfish are among the most unusual fish in the sea. These bony fish have oval-shaped bodies and no tails. Their mouths resemble beaks.

Most ocean sunfish are about as tall as they are long. The smallest are about two feet (1 m) long. The largest can measure more than 11 feet (3 m)!

FAST FACTS

Ocean sunfish are the heaviest bony fish in the world. The average ocean sunfish weighs 2,200 pounds (1,000 kg)!

Most ocean sunfish are pale gray or brown. But, some have bold light and dark patterns.

Ocean sunfish live in **tropical** and **temperate** ocean waters. These large, slow creatures spend much of their time around coral **reefs**. Sometimes they float near the surface, too.

An ocean sunfish is sometimes mistaken for a shark. This happens when its top fin breaks the surface.

A Closer Look

An ocean sunfish's skin is thick and rough. It is covered with **mucus** and toothlike scales called denticles.

Most bony fish have tailbones. But, an ocean sunfish's rear is rounded and ends with a clavus. The clavus helps an ocean sunfish steer while swimming.

FAST FACTS

On some areas of its body, an ocean sunfish's skin may be three inches (8 cm) thick!

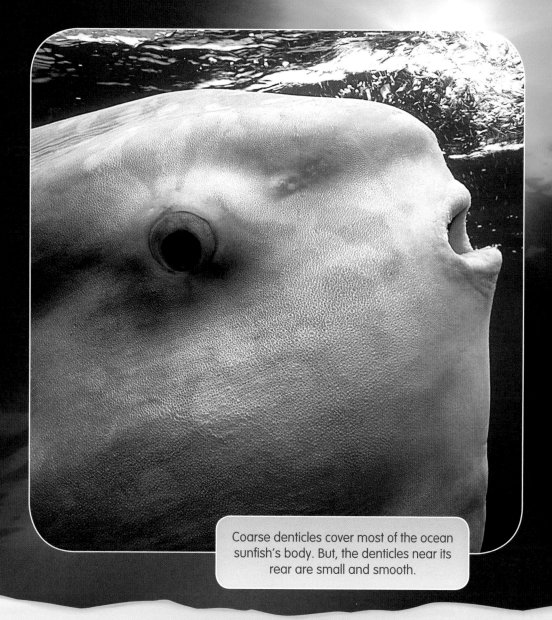

Coarse denticles cover most of the ocean sunfish's body. But, the denticles near its rear are small and smooth.

An ocean sunfish has two long fins. These fins help it move through the water. The dorsal fin is on the top of its body. The anal fin is on the bottom. An ocean sunfish also has a very small pectoral fin on each side of its body.

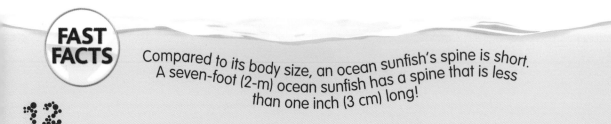

FAST FACTS

Compared to its body size, an ocean sunfish's spine is short. A seven-foot (2-m) ocean sunfish has a spine that is less than one inch (3 cm) long!

The Body Of An Ocean Sunfish

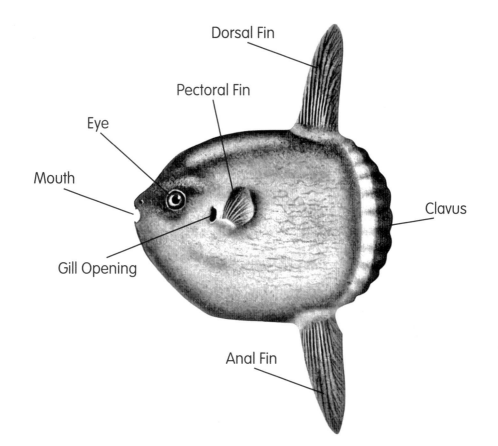

Dorsal Fin

Pectoral Fin

Eye

Mouth

Clavus

Gill Opening

Anal Fin

Three Species

There are three **species** of ocean sunfish in our underwater world. Two grow to be quite large.

Round-tailed and sharp-tailed ocean sunfish can grow more than ten feet (3 m) long. The slender ocean sunfish is the smallest species. It only grows to about two feet (1 m) in length.

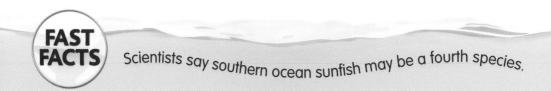

FAST FACTS Scientists say southern ocean sunfish may be a fourth species.

16

Divers most often see the round-tailed, or common, ocean sunfish.

The slender ocean sunfish is more colorful than other ocean sunfish.

The sharp-tailed ocean sunfish's clavus has a pointy extension.

A Growing Ocean Sunfish

Ocean sunfish begin their lives as tiny eggs. A female scatters her eggs in the water. They drift and float until a male **fertilizes** them.

When they hatch, young ocean sunfish are very small. But as they grow, their weight will increase 60 million times!

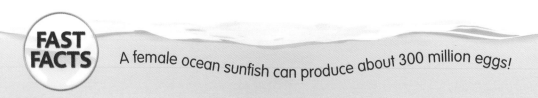

FAST FACTS A female ocean sunfish can produce about 300 million eggs!

Ocean sunfish larvae go through many changes as they grow.

Family Connections

Ocean sunfish belong to a group of fish that includes puffer fish and porcupine fish. This group also includes triggerfish, boxfish, and filefish. They all have four fused teeth that form a beaklike mouth.

Colorful triggerfish live in shallow tropical waters.

A filefish has tiny, spiny scales covering its body. These make the fish's skin feel like sandpaper.

When in trouble, porcupine fish can swim into narrow places. There they puff up their bodies. Then, their spines lock them in place.

Puffer fish can blow up like balloons when threatened by predators.

Boxfish are also known as trunkfish or cowfish. Their bodies are protected by a hard covering called a carapace.

Dinnertime

Ocean sunfish mostly feed on soft-bodied creatures. But, they also eat a variety of small plants and animals. Their diet includes **crustaceans** and **mollusks**. Some ocean sunfish eat **zooplankton**, sea sponges, and eelgrasses.

An ocean sunfish breaks its food into small pieces with its tough beak. It sucks and spits the food until it can be swallowed.

Ocean sunfish eat both comb jellies *(above)* and jellyfish *(right)*.

An ocean sunfish has rough, toothlike **barbs** in its throat. These also help it break up and swallow prey.

Ocean sunfish find food throughout the ocean. They feed among floating weeds near the surface. They also hunt on the seafloor and in the deep ocean.

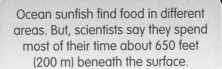

Ocean sunfish find food in different areas. But, scientists say they spend most of their time about 650 feet (200 m) beneath the surface.

A World Of Danger

Ocean sunfish face a variety of threats. One of the most common threats is **parasites**.

More than 40 different parasites are known to bother these gentle fish. Some parasites attach themselves to an ocean sunfish's skin. Others live in its stomach.

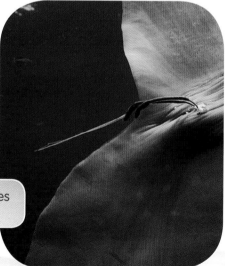

Parasites can cause illnesses in ocean sunfish.

FAST FACTS

Ocean sunfish have been seen jumping out of the water. Scientists say they do this to knock parasites off their skin.

Ocean sunfish visit areas where wrasse fish live. These tiny fish eat parasites living on ocean sunfish and clean their bodies.

Gill nets are another serious danger to ocean sunfish. Fishermen use them to catch thresher sharks and swordfish. But, the nets also trap and harm many ocean sunfish.

Ocean sunfish swim near the water's surface each night. Often, this is when they get caught in gill nets.

Some people in Japan and Taiwan consider ocean sunfish a special meal.

Sea lions *(left)* and orcas *(below)* eat adult ocean sunfish.

Ocean sunfish also have few natural predators. Bluefin tuna and mahi mahi prey on younger ocean sunfish. Larger predators hunt adult ocean sunfish.

Fascinating Facts

▶ California's Monterey Bay Aquarium had an ocean sunfish that outgrew its aquarium. It gained more than 800 pounds (360 kg) in 14 months! Biologists moved the ocean sunfish back to the sea using a helicopter.

This ocean sunfish weighed 57 pounds (2 kg) when caught by Monterey Bay Aquarium staff. It weighed 880 pounds (399 kg) when released.

🍂 Biologist Carl Linnaeus gave the ocean sunfish the scientific name *Mola* in the 1700s. *Mola* is Latin for "millstone." Ocean sunfish reminded Linnaeus of the rough gray stones used in grain mills.

🍂 In France and Spain, ocean sunfish are known as moonfish. In Germany, they are named swimming head fish. And in Taiwan, they are called toppled car fish.

Learn And Explore

Marine biologist Tierney Thys uses special tags to study ocean sunfish. Each tag tracks a fish for two years. Then, it pops off and floats to the surface.

The tag's information is sent to Thys's computer. The data tells fishermen where ocean sunfish are. This helps fisherman reduce the amount of ocean sunfish that are caught accidentally.

Thys and her team have tagged ocean sunfish near California, Japan, Taiwan, Australia, and South Africa.

IMPORTANT WORDS

barb a sharp projection that extends backward and prevents easy removal.

crustacean any of a group of animals with hard shells that live mostly in water. Crabs, lobsters, and shrimp are all crustaceans.

fertilize to make fertile. Something that is fertile is capable of growing or developing.

marine of or relating to the sea.

mollusk an animal with a soft, unsegmented body without a backbone. Snails, clams, and squid are all mollusks.

mucus thick, slippery fluid from the body.

parasite an organism that lives off of another organism of a different species.

reef an underwater ridge of rock, coral, or sand.

species living things that are very much alike.

temperate having neither very hot nor very cold weather.

tropical having warm temperatures.

zooplankton small animals that float in a body of water.

WEB SITES

To learn more about ocean sunfish, visit ABDO Publishing Company on the World Wide Web. Web sites about ocean sunfish are featured on our Book Links page. These links are routinely monitored and updated to provide the most current information available.

www.abdopublishing.com

INDEX

Australia **30**

clavus **10, 13, 15**

color **7, 15**

denticles **10, 11**

eggs **16**

enemies **24, 25, 26, 27**

eye **13**

fin **9, 12, 13**

food **20, 21, 22, 23**

France **29**

Germany **29**

gill opening **13**

habitat **4, 6, 8, 22, 23, 26**

Japan **26, 30**

life cycle **16, 17**

Linnaeus, Carl **29**

mouth **6, 13, 18, 20**

mucus **10**

parasites **24, 25**

relatives **18, 19**

round-tailed
  ocean sunfish **14, 15**

shape **6, 10, 15**

sharp-tailed
  ocean sunfish **14, 15**

size **6, 8, 12, 14, 16, 28**

skin **10, 24**

slender ocean sunfish **14, 15**

South Africa **30**

southern ocean sunfish **14**

Spain **29**

Taiwan **26, 29, 30**

teeth **18**

throat **21**

Thys, Tierney **30**

United States **28, 30**